MORE GREAT QUESTIONS!

*Reflections on Career Navigation,
Professional Courage, and
Project Management Wisdom*

BILL SMILLIE

ISBN: 978-1-4834-7873-9 (sc)
ISBN: 978-1-4834-7872-2 (e)

Lulu Publishing Services rev. date: 12/28/2017

ACKNOWLEDGEMENTS

I heard someone say once, with regard to the profession of consulting, that everything we know that is of any value we learned from a client. The real point being we learn while serving clients, and so we owe them a debt of gratitude.

I have also learned a huge amount from my colleagues and my IBM Cornerstone participants with whom I have had the pleasure to work. They are far too numerous to mention individually, but they have changed my thinking, and that is a gift to be treasured.

And most significantly, I am deeply grateful to my wife Linda, who let me go off and play and learn in the name of working and supporting my family. Throughout my career, when she or my children were asked what it was that I do, they never knew quite what to say. I guess they could have said that I was out there with clients and colleagues learning how to ask great questions.

PREFACE TO MORE GREAT QUESTIONS!

It has been more than half a decade since the first Great Question! publication came into print. It therefore seemed an appropriate time to compile this update to reflect my more recent musings and learning. Much of this newer content is the result of my participation in designing and delivering IBM's remarkably effective Cornerstone program, which accelerates senior consultants to the executive level. This work has not only been extraordinarily fulfilling, it has stimulated my thinking about the three main themes of this sequel – Career Navigation, Professional Courage, and Project Management Wisdom.

Some of this material is repeated from the original publication, in order to create what I consider to be a more coherent view of the topic. All of the ideas reflect my ongoing efforts to make sense and see the bigger picture as I navigated through my professional life. My hope is that I will make some contribution to your thinking as well.

CONTENTS

FINDING THE RIGHT QUESTIONS

The philosopher Kierkegaard said, "Life can only be understood backwards, but it must be lived forwards."

This concept certainly applies to our professional lives. How many times have you heard: "If I only knew then what I know now"? It's taken me decades of pursuing a career for me to be in a position to offer these thoughts. It's a hard-won perspective—and I'm glad to share it. I hope it saves you a decade or two.

There's nothing I like better than the provocation of a great question. I like to have my thinking shifted, and I like to create new frames for thinking about things. I believe that the deepest learning comes from change—and vice versa. In either case, I think a powerful question is a great place to start.

And so, to that end, I have collected a few reflections from my experiences as a project/program leader, as a management consultant, and as a designer and facilitator of professional development programs. These reflections are framed by questions, and are organized into the broad topics of career navigation, professional courage, and project management wisdom.

There is no need to read these in any special order. They largely stand on their own. You can digest them individually, in twos and threes, or altogether at some longer sitting. Just check out the Table of Contents and find a question that grabs you.

And see if your thinking gets changed.

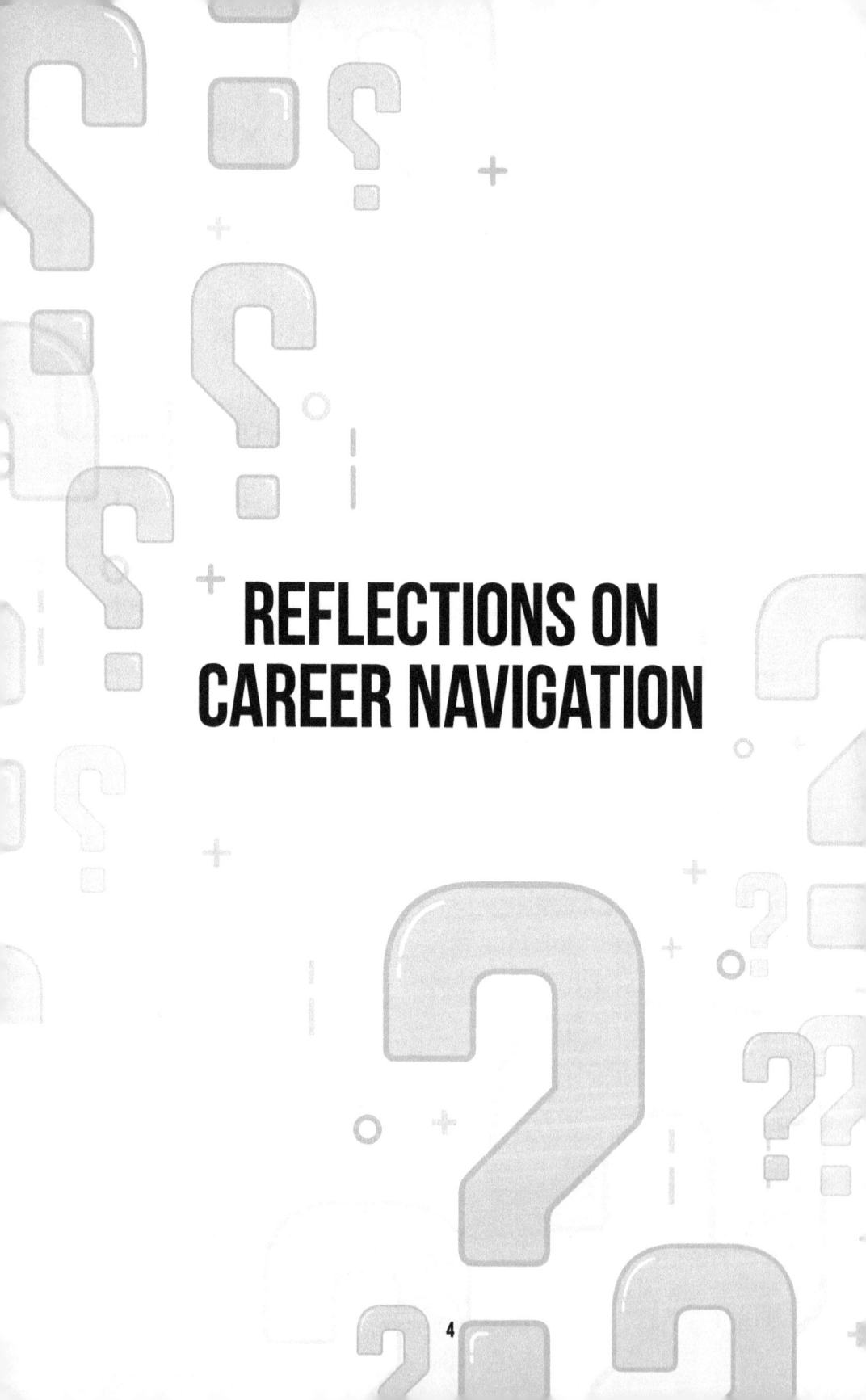

REFLECTIONS ON
CAREER NAVIGATION

WHAT DOES IT MEAN TO BE "PROFESSIONAL"?

Whether we are advising clients or our own senior management, whether we are in the role of strategist, planner, marketer, seller, developer, implementer, or general manager, we are called upon to act and behave "professionally." So, what does that mean, and more interestingly, how can we grow in this important aspect of our careers?

I think about professionalism in three fundamental dimensions: presence, values, and intellect. And I think it is entirely possible to grow in each of these aspects over the course of a career.

Presence is the most straightforward dimension and the easiest to master. At the simplest level, this means not slurping our soup. It means showing up on time and dressing appropriately. It means treating everyone with courtesy and respect. There is a form of professional behavior for virtual interaction as well, or what I have described elsewhere as one's Virtual Intelligence Quotient (VQ).

Beyond these aspects of presence, there is that wonderful phrase "executive presence". When you ask some people for a definition, you get a version of the quote from former Supreme Court Justice Potter Stewart about pornography: "I can't define it but I know it when I see it." I believe executive presence is definable *and learnable*. It comes from being interesting to those who hold executive positions. That requires being curious about people and the issues in their professional and personal lives. It requires having a point of view that stimulates discussion and exchange of ideas. And it requires the confidence to be authentic—not someone you're not, but the humorous, interesting, emotional, fallible, unique person you are. All those elements of executive presence can be practiced and refined by any of us who choose to hone this dimension of our professionalism.

Values represent a more nebulous dimension, because

situations—and our behavioral response to them—are rarely categorized in purely black and white terms. As professionals, though, we are called upon to behave truthfully and courageously. We should be prepared to say what people *need* to hear, not simply what they *want* to hear. And we must do so constructively and tactfully, often in the face of subtle or not so subtle pressure to go along with the crowd or not make waves.

There are generally four stakeholders who must be served by our values: our clients, our company, our people, and our selves. The moral and ethical dilemmas we will face are those in which one stakeholder's interests are in conflict with another's. We may face situations, over the course of our careers, when we are pressured to do the expedient thing, not the right thing. In many of those situations, the only real choice we have is whether we make a career decision early, or whether we will be forced to make one later, but we will be making a career decision. We can and must learn to recognize those situations and act early and professionally.

And finally, there is the dimension of intellect. Sometimes this is referred to as thought leadership. One organization I know is using the term "eminence." Both terms imply that we must do two things.

The first is to have a point of view. It is not enough to merely be smart. You have to be smart about something, in a way that not many others around you are. You must use your smarts to develop insight.

Second, it's not enough to have insights if no one knows you have them. "Thought leadership" implies that you are operating in some arena and in some fashion to have people perceive you as an intellectual leader. "Eminence" implies that some audience has deemed you as being distinguished in some field. So, we need to learn how to convince others we have something to offer intellectually.

In fact, this is not so hard to do. There is usually some local chapter of some related professional organization that would be willing to let you speak at their next meeting. Or, perhaps, there is a professional publication for which you could write an article, or at least a letter to the editor. Within our organizations, there is likely some form of a knowledge management function that would be delighted to receive a submission describing some best practice or sample product. And these days it is becoming important to have "digital eminence," perhaps through a blog or Twitter account.

Yes, but what if we do that, and someone finds a hole in our argument, or points out some aspect that we hadn't fully considered? That, in fact, is the real beauty of the dimension of intellect. Every time we get a response like that to our point of view, we have an opportunity to build a better, more robust one, in a way we couldn't if we just sat by ourselves and contemplated our professional navel.

And so, I come back to my contention that in each of these three dimensions of professionalism, we *can* aspire to achieve new levels of behavior and performance. It just takes a bit of self-awareness and a willingness to work at it.

As I reiterate later, one useful model for learning in a professional environment is this:

- To change business performance, you must change behavior
- To change behavior, you must change thinking
- To change thinking, you must change beliefs and assumptions.

The fundamental first step in this journey is awareness. Seek out those people and those experiences that create self-awareness and you are well on your way to changing your professional performance.

WHY SHOULD YOU CARE ABOUT PERSONAL BRANDING?

What is all the fuss about personal branding? When I Googled "personal branding." I got 6,570,000 hits! Is this simply the latest narcissistic fad? Or is it relevant to our professional lives? And should you even try to blend your work and your life in your personal brand?

The questions intrigued me, so I went looking for insights into how to express a personal brand. This is the most useful description I found:

"To crystallize your personal brand, ask yourself what you want to be known for—what differentiates you from everyone else who might have a similar background or set of experiences? In other words, what skills, abilities, knowledge, and attitudes do you have (or are developing) that will make people want to work with, follow, or 'friend' you—online or off? What value can you create for others as a friend, blogger, colleague, teammate, boss, or subordinate? And what will make you satisfied and fulfilled that you are indeed making a contribution?"

And...

"Your brand can also aspire to describe who you are; what you stand for; what makes you unique, special, and different; and what your values are."

I have recently been working with high-performing senior professionals who are striving to build a higher level of competence in leadership while struggling to find balance in their lives. This challenge of reaching for personal growth has led me to embrace the process of developing a personal brand. And, yes, the process of *articulating* a personal brand may be as valuable as actually having one. Want to see why? Try completing the following three sentences (and I mean sentences, not paragraphs):

I am (or am becoming)…
I believe…
I will…

I would be willing to bet you did not find this an easy exercise to complete. I would be further willing to bet that when you did complete it, the process actually changed your thinking. And if you really want to stretch yourself and push your thinking, I suggest you share this work with a trusted advisor and ask them to challenge your statements in terms of a sound balance between growth and fulfillment.

WHAT IS YOUR VQ (VIRTUAL INTELLIGENCE QUOTIENT)?

As our work worlds increasingly require us to interact across time and distance, Virtual Intelligence is the latest in the multiple intelligences we are being asked to master. Here is a quick—totally unscientific—self-assessment you can apply to the way you work in virtual settings. Rate yourself on a scale of 1 to 10 for each of the 16 questions. A score of 160 means you have self-assessed at a genius level with respect to your VQ.

<u>Virtual Professional Appearance (maximum 20 points)</u>

1. Do you have a good quality picture of yourself – a "head" shot, not one of you in front of Niagara Falls, riding your motorcycle, or holding your favorite pet - in all the software (e.g. MS Outlook, instant messaging applications) and sites (e.g. Plaxo, Linked In) that you use?
2. Does your signature block contain all appropriate contact information (and do you avoid extraneous and cutesy quotations and sayings)?

Virtual Work Place Behavior (maximum 50 points)

3. Are you always cognizant of the difference in time zones between you and the people you are working with?
4. Do you avoid sending gratuitous emails (such as the joke of the day, or superfluous "thanks" in a reply-to-all)?
5. Do you avoid attaching large files, or when that becomes necessary, do you send a warning in advance?
6. Do you respond in a timely manner (never taking longer than 48 hours)?
7. Do you make every effort to learn and properly use the collaboration technology adopted by your team?

Virtual Meeting Behavior (maximum 60 points)

8. Do you appropriately announce your presence and avoid anonymous lurking?
9. Do you – without fail – arrive on time?
10. Are you sensitive to not introducing extraneous noise (e.g. no teleconferences while ordering lunch)?
11. Do you intentionally avoid or minimize multi-tasking and/or concurrent IM gossiping?
12. Do you conscientiously prepare by studying the material sent to you in advance?
13. Do you join the conversation, making thoughtful contributions?

Virtual Leadership Behavior (maximum 30 points)

14. Do people know where you want to go (do you set agendas in advance)?
15. Do you give people an appropriate sense of your personality and humanity (e.g. do you show a sense of humor, of passion, of curiosity, of a positive frame of mind)?

16. Do you first assume positive intent (there must be a valid reason for their behavior, and I should not respond negatively, even if I am inclined to do so, until I have all the facts)?

WHO'S ON YOUR PERSONAL "BOARD OF DIRECTORS"?

It seems to me that the notion of governance can be applied to one's personal and professional development. Just as in other applications of a governance model, we can benefit from an oversight that is focused on our personal and professional direction and strategy. This oversight is also concerned about our sustainability, and provides a mechanism for accountability of actions and outcomes. And like good governance models, this oversight does not take responsibility for execution. That is up to management or, in the case of our own development, we are the ones who are solely and personally responsible.

How then might you think about what kinds of "directors" you would invite onto your personal "board"?

Here are what I believe to be the three essential roles:

- The Mentor, who is a door-opener, who provides access to a network, and who is a role model we would like to emulate in some way;
- The Trusted Advisor, who is a counselor, who has wisdom and experience to impart, and who will tell us what we need to hear—even if it's not what we want to hear; and, finally,
- The Coach, and not the sports model of coach who calls the plays, but the therapist/listener/reflector model of coach, who lets us gain access to our inner wisdom, and helps us manage our internal saboteur.

No one can play all three roles, although some can be both Mentor and Trusted Advisor, or Trusted Advisor and Coach. It may be difficult for a Mentor to have enough detachment from his or her protégé to be their Coach as well. And of course, one's personal "board" can and typically should have more than one of each. So, who's on your board of directors? Who should be on your board but hasn't yet been recruited?

Don't you think the "Enterprise of You" deserves the best possible governance?

HOW DO YOU MANAGE A CAREER IF CAREER PLANNING DOESN'T WORK?

At no time in my career could I have predicted, five years previously, where I was going to be or what I was going to be doing. That statement is true for me (across the span of a forty year career), and I believe it is true for most, if not all, professionals. Terrific! So, career management is like betting at the roulette table? Or perhaps like the ball in a pinball machine – Fate pulls back the plunger and you and your career go ricocheting wildly off the bumpers and paddles until you finally fall down the hole in the bottom, only to return to the plunger once more. Yikes!

Fortunately, no. It is true that specific steps and assignments cannot be accurately planned far in advance. But there is a push-pull strategy that can be used to accelerate career advancement. It involves the pull of a network of mentors/sponsors and the push of a personal desire to stretch into new competencies and expertise.

Linda A. Hill, a Harvard Business School Professor who has done extensive research in this area, has articulated one model for this strategy. She describes a repeating cycle in which a stretch opportunity is orchestrated through a personal network resulting in new competencies and a more prominent reputation. All of which leads to a more powerful network that helps provide the next stretch opportunity, and so on.

That would explain why accurately predicting the next five years isn't possible. But what would make it intentional and what would make it happen faster rather than slower? I believe the answer lies in what we choose to do in growing our networks and in pushing ourselves to stretch. Elsewhere I have written about one's Personal Board of Directors. This concept involves intentionally recruiting mentors/sponsors (the pull side of the strategy to find stretch opportunities) as well as trusted advisors and coaches (the push side of the strategy to help understand the necessary areas for growth and to embrace the challenge of stretching).

In the final analysis, you can't plan a career far in advance. You can, however, put in place your own mechanisms to build competency and reputation. Do that, and the rewarding career will follow. It's a sure bet.

WHAT DOES IT TAKE TO SURVIVE AND THRIVE IN TODAY'S PROFESSIONAL SERVICES ORGANIZATIONS?

[The following is particularly relevant to for-profit consultancies, but can be applied to public sector and non-profit organizations if you substitute "mission objectives" for "financial objectives".]

In terms of serving your masters, your client comes first.

Right behind this obligation, though, is the pressure to serve your organization. And senior management is very focused on signings, revenue, and profitability, as they should be, given their responsibility to shareholders and to the bottom line.

That focus is manifested through the systems that measure progress to targets, which often result in last-minute calls to action and significant amounts of your time away from your clients while receiving "help" from senior management.

And that "help" is almost never helpful, because of two realities:

- With respect to <u>both</u> your sales and your delivery, the critical drivers of your performance are not measurable by those management systems, and
- Those performance drivers cannot be put in place at the last minute, regardless of how much you or your senior management wish it were so.

How, then, can you survive and thrive in today's challenging professional services environment?

The simple answer is to never need that kind of "help".

The less obvious answer is to act based on what you <u>believe</u> about your long-term investments that are necessary to drive your future short-term successes.

What are the drivers of long-term performance in signings, profit, talent development, and personal renewal? What should you believe is <u>important</u> personal behavior, in spite of the <u>urgent</u> messages coming from "the system"? What <u>personal</u> management system will you have to implement in order to sustain that behavior?

Figure that out, and you will not only survive, you will thrive in your chosen career.

HOW CAN YOU TAKE ADVANTAGE OF ORGANIZATIONAL CHANGE?

Oh, no. Yet another org change! Just when you finally got comfortable with your role/boss/colleagues. How can you turn this from threat to opportunity? By accepting the fact that it probably means *you* need to change as well.

"In what way should I change?" you ask. "And what will it mean to my career?" "What's going on in this organization anyway?" Great questions, wrong sequence.

The way to deal with organizational change is to first understand why the organization is changing. Odds are that your organization is responding to changes in its environment. Clients are asking for different services and solutions. Competitors are changing. Technology is changing (duh!). And of course, everyone is being affected by the economy.

So, answer these questions, in this order:

- Why is my organization changing (at the business unit level)?
- What does my organization need to succeed (at the profit center level)?
- Where would my organization benefit from some leadership and vision (at the group level)?
- How do I need to change and grow to provide that leadership and vision?

The way to change this personal threat into a personal opportunity is to start with the big picture first and make the personal decisions within that context. Then go for it!

WHERE IS YOUR PROFESSIONAL SWEET SPOT?

Consider three dimensions of work: what you know a lot about (the source of your wisdom), what you love to do (the source of your passion, or "psychic compensation"), and how you want to engage and be engaged (your "terms and conditions") for working. Your sweet spot is defined by where they overlap.

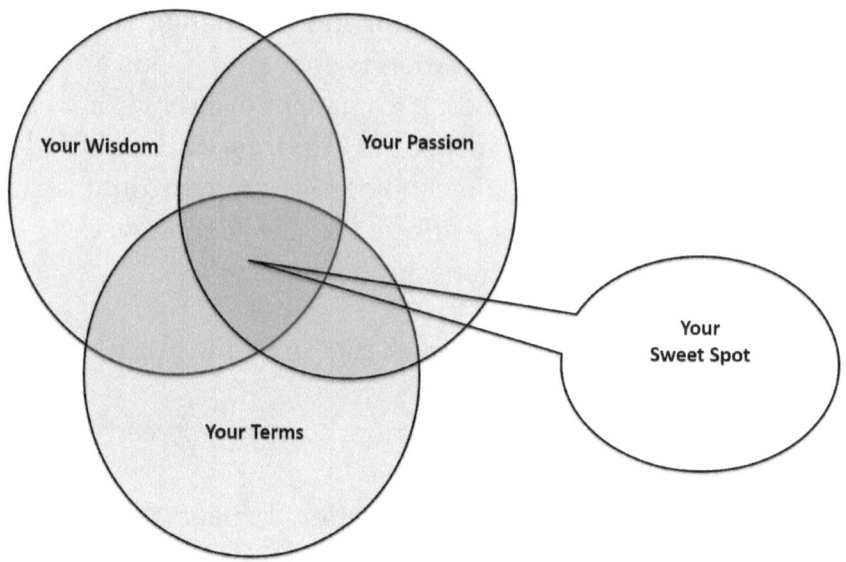

Now create those three lists for yourself. Here's mine:

- Wisdom
    - Growing and sustaining profitable professional services businesses
    - Designing and delivering professional development programs
    - Understanding what it takes to be an expert project or programme manager
    - Knowing what best practices are critical to non-profit Boards
- Passion
    - Being a change agent
    - Being a coach/facilitator/provocateur
    - Collaborating with trusted and respected colleagues
    - Stretching and learning, for myself and with others

- Terms
  - Independence
  - Part-time, or full-time for a limited duration
  - Only traveling internationally if in business class
  - Having fun.

Now think about when in your professional life those three areas overlapped, because that is your sweet spot.

In my case, two stand out:

- working with – or on – non-profit Boards in Baltimore, and
- designing and delivering professional development programs for professionals on an executive track.

So where is your sweet spot? What were you doing when you were in your sweet spot? Where will you go for your next sweet spot adventure? What will you do to make it happen?

REFLECTIONS ON PROFESSIONAL COURAGE

WHAT IS YOUR MORAL COMPASS FOR NAVIGATING CORPORATE LIFE?

Here's a scenario: your company is counting on you to profitably deliver an outcome for which your client has agreed to pay a great deal, and upon which your client's business performance is heavily dependent. If you perform well, you will be rewarded with a significant promotion. Your team, and especially the key players who have been working overtime for the last 6 months, have advised that a 2-month delay in the schedule will be necessary. This will delay the client's business benefit and will negatively affect the profitability of the contract.

Whose interests are paramount? To whom do you owe the greatest loyalty: your client, your company, your people, or yourself? How do you make that decision?

At any level of management, including the executive levels, and in almost any kind of business, we are tasked to do four things:

- Bring value to our clients or customers
- Bring value to our company
- Bring value to the people we lead and influence
- Bring value to our career and ourselves.

Indeed, what differentiates the role of a manager versus a director versus an entry-level executive versus a senior executive is defined by the scope of responsibilities in each of those four areas.

And moral dilemmas are defined and created by the potential conflict between two or more of those areas. In fact, the scenario described above has all four in play. So what would you do? More interestingly, how would you decide?

I don't claim to have all the answers, or even to have always behaved over the course of my career to the highest moral standards. Here is what I do believe.

First, you must do your best to decide what is "truth" in any given circumstance. In the above example, you would need to realistically assess the feasibility of adhering to the original schedule. Can it be done at all by anyone? Can this team do it? What will be the human cost, if it is in fact feasible? What will the business cost be to the client if there is a planned 2-month delay? What will the business cost be to the client, the company, and the people if there is an <u>unplanned</u> 2-month delay? I am reminded of a line from the recent movie, "Margin Call" when, as the investment company's world begins to crumble, and the executive in charge of risk management is recalling a key decision of the previous year, she reflects, "It seemed like the only choice at the time." The truth, if it were to be analyzed dispassionately, invariably suggests multiple choices.

Next, I believe our professional obligations generally should be prioritized in the order of client over company over people over oneself. Why? Clients come first because we, as individuals and as enterprises, cannot endure if we do otherwise. The company comes second, because we have an employment contract to honor, based upon which we are being paid to help the company achieve its goals. And our people come before us, because we cannot sustain a leadership role if people believe we will put our self-interests before theirs.

Some have argued that if we put our people first, the rest will fall into place. I agree that employee engagement is a key driver of business results, and much of our leadership energies should be focused there. But that shouldn't change the rank ordering of our moral obligations, and as leaders we should make sure that our teams share the same understanding.

And finally, no matter which area is given preference in any specific circumstance, it should never be at the total expense of any one of the parties. Any such decision tends to suggest coercion or bullying, in my experience. While a "win-win" solution may not be possible in every case, there is almost always a way forward that does not involve totally "throwing under the bus" any one area of interest.

One final point: I do believe that client interests come first, but if one is confident they will be reasonably addressed, then one can go to the next perspective down the chain, and so forth. Of course, one's thinking is typically not as sequential as that – it often is quite iterative. But the notion of the hierarchy still seems to me like a good approach to navigating the waters.

So the next time you feel at risk of getting lost in the murky morality of corporate life, I suggest you start with the truth, and then decide whose interests should come in what order, while finding some way to acknowledge all the perspectives.

It won't make your days simpler, but it might make your nights a lot more restful.

WILL YOU SPEAK TRUTH TO POWER?

Your boss just recommended the dumbest idea. Worse yet, the Senior Vice President - for whom you are slated to lead her key strategic initiative - just demanded an implementation schedule that is unrealistic. Your boss's boss just asked you to fill a key role on your team with his inexperienced protégé.

There is enough power-related insanity in the bigger world these days. Now it seems to be invading your own working world.

Yikes! What to do?

Well, not to belabor the obvious, but you have two choices: acquiesce, or object.

Your first thought is to acquiesce, because not to do so would be a CLM (career limiting move).

But here's my thought for your consideration. Sometimes, life gives you only two choices: make a potential career-changing decision now, or have an actual one made for you later.

One thing is certain. People who ask you to do the impossible don't know as much – and aren't as experienced – as you are in the specific domain under discussion. Furthermore, it is entirely likely that if they are pushed (e.g. you say that you can't be successful, but perhaps they can find someone else who will), they will quickly re-evaluate and back off their demands.

On the other hand, they may not, and will punish you for insubordination. Now there's an alternate universe that seems highly unattractive!

So when your gut tells you it is wrong, know that you have the hard-earned experience to be confident that you are right!

Do you want to make a choice now, or have one made for you later?

Simple choice, but not an easy decision. True for project managers, and now, apparently, true for citizens and elected officials.

WHAT DO AMBIGUOUS THREATS AND RECOVERY WINDOWS HAVE TO DO WITH COURAGEOUS PROJECT MANAGEMENT?

The Columbia space shuttle disaster of 2003 provided a particularly poignant example for some work done at the Harvard Business School by Amy C. Edmundson, Michael A. Roberto, and Richard M. J. Bohmer[1]. The loss of the ship and all crewmembers was found to be the result of a foam strike upon launch. There had been a twenty-year history of such strikes, although this one appeared to be a particularly large piece that may have been capable of causing structural damage. Asking the CIA to divert some spy satellites to take pictures of the exterior of the shuttle, and ultimately launching a rescue shuttle, would have been the only decisions that might have altered the course of this particular history. No one seemed individually prepared to argue strongly for either action. When the decision was made to wait until after re-entry to complete the examination, the fate of the crew was sealed.

What has this got to do with courageous project management?

The Harvard researchers described two phenomena in decision-making within organizations: ambiguous threats – risks that may have an outcome that is completely unacceptable – and recovery windows – that period of time beyond which no recovery is possible, regardless of subsequent actions.

Does that sound familiar in the project management world? Looking back on disasters we have been close to, wasn't it obvious that success was unobtainable unless the poor estimate, inadequate team skills, lack of key sponsorship, or whatever other critical factor was in play had been addressed early and quickly?

I have written before on the topic of speaking truth to power. Let me explore one aspect of the dynamics at play – the apparent powerlessness that project managers feel they face.

Typically, executives are placing direct or indirect coercive pressure on project managers to "just do it". And yet, I believe that it is the project manager with a track record of successful delivery who holds the real power. Imagine the response if any of us were to stand up and say, "I cannot be successful unless we take the following actions within this specific time frame. If that can't happen, you need to find a project manager who you believe can do it. I am not that person." I believe that nine times out of ten, the executives will respond as we need them to, because they know in their fat little hearts that we are right. In the case of the other one time, we don't want to be anywhere near the pending disaster anyway.

Acting courageously is easier when you know you're right and you know you have power. As you think about your next project, evaluate the ambiguous threats, determine the recovery window for corrective actions, and know that you are the power player in altering the course of this project's history.

---

[1] "Facing ambiguous threats" Roberto, Michael A;
Bohmer, Richard M J; Edmundson, Amy C
Harvard Business Review
November 2006 pp106,108-113

REFLECTIONS ON PROJECT MANAGEMENT WISDOM

WHAT IS THE DIFFERENCE BETWEEN A PROJECT MANAGER AND A PROGRAM LEADER?

That would beg the question of what the difference is between a project and a program (or programme, as many of my international colleagues would spell it). Programs, unlike projects, are, by intention, transformational. As a consequence, here are some characteristics of programs that are different from projects:

- The stakeholder landscape includes board level and cross-functional senior executives
- The nature of a program is often a "bet the company" strategic effort
- The specific work plan is not knowable at the beginning of the journey
- Expanding value delivered is more critical than controlling scope
- The performance of a team of hundreds (not dozens) needs inspirational (not controlling) styles of leadership
- The solutions that leverage such significant business value have many potential failure points
- The organizations responsible for delivery (internal IT, software vendors, consultancies) must also adopt a "bet the company" level of commitment.

(Some of you may have noticed that the previous seven bullet points seem curiously correlated to my view of the dimensions of project/program health. No coincidence there.)

So how does that translate into the differences in our personal "game" as we move from project manager to program leader? Here is my view of the critical areas that require a transformation in our own competencies:

- Executive level relationship management—we must become trusted advisors to a wide variety of senior stakeholders
- Leadership and personal power—we must achieve through influence and coaching, not through command and control
- Understanding and delivering business value—we must gain a deep understanding of the business problem, and ensure that all aspects of the program are driving to optimize business value
- Articulating a vision—it is our ability to inspire that will keep everyone moving toward the goal, in spite of fears, anxieties, and confusions that are inherent in programs
- Masterful negotiating skills—we must be able to design a win-win situation among the many (and often competing) internal and external organizational objectives

Sound a bit daunting? Here is the good news: I believe that effective program leaders are made, not born. That is to say, one can learn and acquire proficiency in the competencies I have listed above.

Mind you, these competencies do not come easily or quickly, but there are approaches that will accelerate these aspects of professional development for the program leaders of tomorrow. The investment of time and money required seems appropriate if you're going to "bet the company" on the competency of a program leader.

WHAT ARE THE MOST POWERFUL QUESTIONS FOR SHIFTING ONE'S THINKING ABOUT PROJECT PERFORMANCE?

These are my two favorite questions. They work for many aspects of life, but they are especially useful in project management:

1. How will we know when we are done?
2. How will we know if we have a good answer (outcome), not just any answer (outcome)?

On these two questions hang all the methods, the controls, and the quality.

I spent many years in the role of Quality Assurance Partner. My job was to make sure the right people were doing the right things. (As opposed to quality control, which is making sure things are done right.) In all those years, my team and I never met a lazy project team. Quite the contrary, the project teams we reviewed all were extraordinarily dedicated and hard working. They weren't always clear, I discovered, about what they should be working on, or what the definition of successful completion should be.

These two simple but powerful questions made them stop and think. And if you think about methods, and the plans and quality outcomes they are designed to support, they all can be evaluated from the basis of my two favorite questions.

Think about traditional methods. Here is a simple pictorial for the life cycle (how you will know when you are done) and the quality traceability mechanisms (how you will know you have a good outcome).

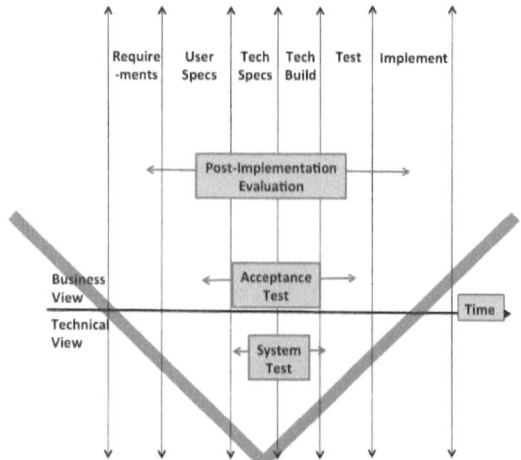

Even the more sophisticated approaches to agile scrum teams can be scrutinized and understood from these same fundamental principles.

Consider the following picture:

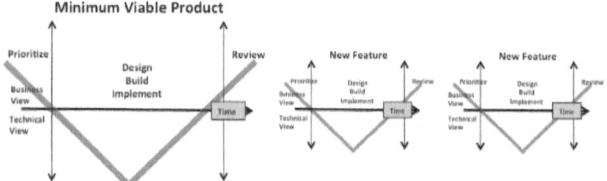

In either case—and I suggest in *any* case—methods and work plans – and good governance - should be designed to help teams answer my two favorite questions. When they do, success is at hand. When they don't, all you can count on is that the team will work hard at something, until sometime.

IF YOU COULD INVENT A VIDEO GAME CALLED PROJECT MANAGEMENT, WHAT WOULD IT BE LIKE?

Here's my version. Imagine this: You, the Project Manager, are at the wheel of a racecar traveling at high speed over open ground. Off in the distance is a wall stretching as far as you can see from left to right, but in the middle of the wall is a hole about twice the width of your car. The challenge is simple. Steer through the hole and you win the prize, and the faster you get there, the bigger the prize. Miss the hole, and you smash into the wall—no prize, no more fast car, no more driver.

So, what's the catch? Well, obviously crosswinds, bumps, loose suspension, and other factors tend to take you off course. All that's fair game. What make this challenge difficult are the following two limitations you must learn to deal with.

First, your steering wheel only turns five degrees left or right—you better be making a lot of small corrections early or you will get yourself to a point where you no longer have room and time to correct.

Second, you can't turn that wheel by yourself—you have a partner in the car with you, your Executive Sponsor, and you only get to make steering corrections if he or she agrees to help. So you better be good at communicating with that sponsor about when steering corrections are required and why.

Does this metaphor for managing projects sound too simple? Of course it is. But I think it's instructive, for three reasons:

1. You must collaborate with your Executive Sponsor in order to take corrective actions.
2. All projects, including successful ones, require lots of corrective actions.
3. This isn't as simple as steering one car toward one hole in the wall. You have to manage (or steer) seven different kinds of vehicles simultaneously if you want to grab

that prize and avoid crashes. That is, I believe there are seven dimensions of project health you need to be continuously monitoring.

Do you have the instrumentation to detect distance from center line (and rate of change), distance from "the wall" (and rate of change), and whether enough time remains for a five-degree correction to take effect?

If not, you're driving blind, wondering when your screen will say, "Game Over!"

HOW CAN YOU ALTER THE COURSE OF HISTORY IN YOUR PROJECT OR PROGRAM?

The number one reason for project failures according to Gartner Group, The Project Management Institute, and many other observers of project management performance is due to issues surrounding executive commitment and sponsorship. Projects—and project management—are now the stuff of boardroom agendas, and we must be good at working those agendas.

How then can we communicate better at the boardroom level? How can we use that communication to get decisions and actions that will guide our projects toward a successful outcome? There is a language and a technique for history-altering communication that has proven to be highly effective on projects. It was developed as a result of the merger of Price Waterhouse and Coopers & Lybrand project management experiences, and has been adopted by IBM, not just in its Global Business Services unit, but also by the company-wide PM Center of Excellence. When PW and C&L merged, we compared notes from both sides and found that this framework embodied the lessons learned by both organizations, across a very wide range of project size, type, and geographic territory.

Now it is IBM's way of managing project health, and is called "The Seven Keys to Success."

These seven dimensions explain every success—and every failure—I have ever seen or heard about in the world of project and program management:

1. Stakeholders are committed
2. Business benefits will be realized
3. Work and schedule are predictable
4. Scope is realistic and managed
5. Team is high performing
6. [Technical] Risks [of the solution] are mitigated
7. Delivery organization benefits will be realized

Before I go on to explain the Seven Keys, I want you to think about the best project you were ever on or ever heard about. Hold that thought. Now think about the worst "death march" you were ever on or ever heard about. Now keep them both in mind as you contemplate the following dimensions of project health that make up The Seven Keys to Success.

Stakeholders are committed. Here are some of my experiences. On one large systems implementation project I reviewed for a complex, multi-national company, I asked who was on their Steering Committee. The answer: "We don't have one." Eventually, one was formed, but it never had solid influence over the all the geographical heads of business units. The project eventually was cancelled. Here are scenes from two other projects early in my career, which happened to occur back-to-back. One included a CIO who actively worked to see the project fail. He succeeded, and it failed. The other, and the best project I ever managed, was for a client who really made it happen—took responsibility, made tough decisions, took political heat, and truly owned the result. I completely "failed" in one, and was a resounding "success" in the other, all in the space of about a year. Did I change tactics or become a different person? No, in fact my "best" project happened immediately before my "worst" project. That was my first lesson that we as project managers aren't the only ones responsible for project outcomes, good or bad.

Business benefits are realized. Sometimes people get caught up in the events and melodrama of a project, and lose sight of the primary objective. I saw this in a large Enterprise Resource Planning (ERP) project. This project was originally designed as a Year 2000 mitigation tactic: "We don't have the time to correct our old, custom-built core financial applications, so we will replace them with ERP software." Actually that was a sound strategy—if it had been done in time! This organization got so caught up in the politics of agreeing on specifications that they almost didn't make the deadline. In this case, they were yanked back into reality by some emphatic messages at the CEO level of the organization. Other projects have lost their way in terms of business benefits and never gotten back on track. I've seen too many projects that never had a sound business case in the first place, and should have been saved from a premature death by never having been born. Yes, you can even use this framework to judge the health of projects you're only thinking about doing.

Work and schedule are predicted. This is the traditional dimension of health. Otherwise known as "on time and on budget." Now, anyone can tell you when this one is in serious trouble. And by then, of course, it's often too late to recover. The trickier challenge is to know early in the project if it is likely to do well or not. Here, process and discipline are everything. With this type of discipline, there will not be many surprises. (There may be unhappy news, but it won't come as a big surprise to anyone.)

Scope is realistic and managed. Get this one right, and "Work and Schedule Are Predicted" is a lot easier. Get it wrong, and both tend to suffer. I remember one project that got way out of control—from an initial budget of under $20 million to actual results of over $80 million. The company was a regulated power utility, which prided itself on having a gentle and mannered culture. The project was a new customer information system, a very complex undertaking. Successful scope management would have required a project manager "mean as a junkyard dog." Instead, the company named one of its own "gentle" men to the job, and the rest, as they say, is history. We're not talking "scope creep" here—this one galloped out of control. My advice is to learn how to be a mean junkyard dog when necessary and in the nicest professional way, of course.

Team is high performing. This one is often overlooked, and yet can make a huge difference. It's not just about talent and experience, although these are obviously important. Morale, trust, physical environment, reward, and recognition—these are some of the factors that determine sickness or health. I have also learned, first hand, how powerful it can be to have a truly diverse team—diverse in style, in nationality, in gender, in life experience. And I also have learned how hard it can be to bring such a team together, how easy it is to convince yourself to take shortcuts in these efforts, how tiresome it can be to continually display the leadership that binds them together. Don't let that get to you. Fight for diversity and fight for the time and resources to build trust and communications among your team. I guarantee your project performance will benefit.

Technical risks are mitigated. The press has reported on a number of high profile implementations that have gone badly for the companies involved. Orders not processed, inventory not managed, market share lost. The ultimate costs to the business and the shareholders have been huge. Many of these cases involved the "big bang" style of implementation—the quickest way, but the riskiest way. Here's the sanity test for these circumstances: "Don't gamble unless you're prepared to lose." These companies gambled and found out they weren't prepared to lose.

Delivery organization benefits are realized. Finally, behind every project, there is a delivery organization that puts it on the line for project management performance. And I'm not just talking about financial issues. Delivery organizations, whether they are hired consultants or internal IT groups, are trying to enhance reputation, harvest lessons learned, and develop staff with each project. If these aims are kept in sight and continually furthered, the final dimension of project health will be served. If these aims cannot be met, then all parties cannot deem the project a complete success, and the resulting conflict of agendas can be very damaging.

Okay, that's The Seven Keys to Success. The real secret to their usefulness is that they are actionable, and remember that that's what we're after when we communicate with our project sponsors—actions that will alter the course of history.

I've always been taught that when you're preparing for an executive level meeting, ask yourself, "What do I want them to know? What do I want them to decide?" This is exactly what The Seven Keys to Success framework provides as your boardroom level communication technique. Project health, for each key, is described as green, yellow, or red. Green means, "stay the course: no corrective action required." Yellow means, "warning: corrective action required in the near term." Red means "urgent: corrective action required immediately." In other words, yellow and red status reports come with a built-in agenda for taking action.

Now, let's revisit your own projects. Think first about your worst project. How many keys went red? How early? Did the underlying conditions get corrected? I'm guessing that multiple keys went red, did so early in the project, and never recovered. Next, your best project, were the Seven Keys always green? I bet they weren't, but I also bet they didn't stay yellow or red for too long.

Successful projects are never in perfect health at all times. But successful projects always address their health issues promptly and effectively. Use The Seven Keys to Success as a built-in agenda for your regular monthly steering committee meetings. Get those health issues on the table, and get the commitment to take the necessary actions.

WHY DON'T GOOD METHODS PREVENT PROJECT PLANNING FAILURES?

Is there now some scientific thinking to suggest method development is a fool's errand? In his recent book, *Streetlights and Shadows: Searching for the Keys To Adaptive Decision Making*, Gary Klein makes an interesting case. He presents a number of arguments with disparate real world examples to show that the more complex the situation and the more extensively documented the procedure (such as most IT development and implementation methods), the less likely a competent professional will use it, and the more likely that an inexperienced person will perform at a mediocre level at best.

Let's run through that one more time. If the target audience for an IT method is experienced project managers, they probably won't use it. And, if the project manager is inexperienced and the project is a complex one, we are pretty sure that's a recipe for disaster.

Hmmm…maybe we need to re-think this a bit.

Historically, project managers have railed at methodologists for not understanding the complexities of project life. (There is an old joke that asks, "What's the difference between a methodologist and a terrorist?" Answer: "You can sometimes negotiate with a terrorist.") So, when the project manager asks the methodologist, "What's the shortest time that this type of project can be done with acceptable quality under the following circumstances?" The answer often sounds like, "I can't tell you, but you better have these 1200 line items in your work breakdown structure."

Why are we surprised, then, that good methods do not appear to prevent project planning failures? Indeed, my experience suggests that most project managers rarely reference method materials, but they almost always reference work plans from trusted sources (and sometimes the only source they trust is themselves).

The corollary might be: why are we surprised when "bad" methods (like the seductive siren song of Rapid Application Development or Agile Development) are adopted with almost religious fervor and misapplied in complex and mission-critical situations?

So, what's the answer? Well, if we can't get methodologists to adequately address the real world of project management, why don't we educate project managers to have a better understanding of methodology?

I am not arguing that project managers re-invent a method for every project (although many like to do that). I am saying we might limit the prescription of methods to, say, twenty-five tasks (five life cycle phases with five tasks each, perhaps) and then teach project managers to build plans that answer my two favorite questions:

1. How will we know when we are done?
2. How will we know we have a good solution, not just any solution?

This, of course, will necessitate extra effort and intelligence at the planning stages of complex projects.

Oh, right, that could be a good thing...

WHAT IS THE POINT OF REPORTING PROJECT OR PROGRAMME STATUS?

In many organizations, the more visible the status is to higher levels of the organization, the less meaning it has.

Wait...what?

So, if an executive wants to know how a portfolio of projects is doing and which projects might be about to experience challenges, she may be pursuing a lost cause?

Yes, for two reasons. First, many project managers have learned that "yellow light" or "red light" status reports make their lives more difficult with unwanted and generally unhelpful attention. "Green light" status reports, on the other hand, make it easier to focus on productive work, which may allow one to skate through the challenges and end up with a successful outcome. *Maybe. Hopefully.*

Second, as I have written elsewhere, what gets measured and reported in most status reports is rarely of any use in predicting and articulating the need for helpful and timely intervention. In many organizations, even if their status reports were accurate, the "yellow light" and especially the "red light" reports would be describing train wrecks in progress. Executive intervention would likely be too late to alter the course of history.

So, what is an executive responsible for a portfolio to do? And what is a project manager navigating a career to do?

The answer in both cases, I contend, is to be a leader of cultural change. Leading downward, executives need to celebrate and reward those project managers who raise flags and ask for help in a timely fashion. And leading upward, project managers need to report status on the most important and leading indicators of project health, along with their recommendations for corrective action by the appropriate executives.

Without such a culture that clearly values the discussion of timely corrective actions, status reports may be little more than a nuisance to project managers and an empty comfort to portfolio executives.

Not much point to that.

WHAT ARE THE MOST IMPORTANT THINGS TO MEASURE, TRACK, AND MANAGE IN PROJECTS AND PROGRAMS?

Interesting question, but it first requires some insight into what "important" is. Let me suggest two dimensions:

1. The degree of impact something has on our ability to deliver a great outcome, and
2. Whether our assessment of that factor gives us a leading or a lagging indication of success.

Great. We now can look at this topic through the lens of a classic two-by-two matrix, like this:

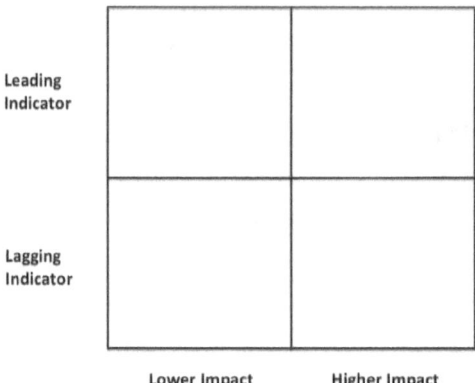

Leading Indicator

Lagging Indicator

Lower Impact   Higher Impact

And we might conclude that the answer to our big question should lie in the upper right quadrant, and secondarily perhaps in the lower right quadrant.

Or are we spending most of our energy on measuring, tracking, and managing other things? Well, let's see.

Elsewhere I have written about seven key factors in project and program success. Briefly, they are:

- Stakeholders are committed
- Business benefits will be realized
- Work and schedule are predictable
- Scope is realistic and managed
- Team is high performing
- Technical risks are mitigated
- Delivery organization benefits will be realized

In my view, and especially as our projects and programs are played for higher and higher stakes, three of those factors are of supreme importance to success:

- Stakeholder commitment
- Business benefits
- High performing team

Furthermore, of the seven factors, only two can truly be assessed in a *leading indicator* fashion (that is, we can have a strong sense of final outcome after less than 10% of budgeted cost and schedule):

- Stakeholder commitment, and
- Business benefits

All others present lagging indications to a greater or lesser degree. That is, by the time enough time has elapsed to give a reliable read out, it can be difficult to "correctably" manage a highly successful outcome.

So, by this analysis, our two-by-two matrix looks like this:

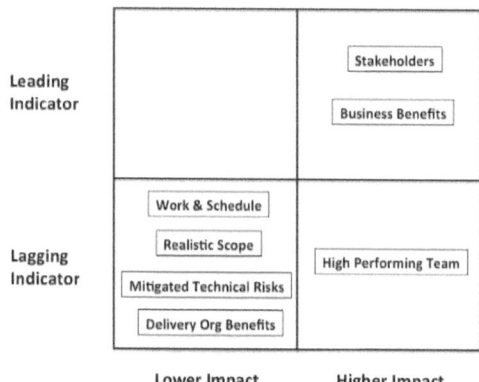

Yet, what do we measure, track, and manage mostly? Things, I suggest, in the lower left quadrant, especially:

- Work & Schedule (although really *only* if we are doing some sort of Earned Value Analysis) and
- Delivery Organization Benefits (and *only* to the extent of understanding the financial costs of delivery versus the promise).

Wait…what? So, we only measure *two* of the seven factors, and those two are *not* the most critical, and in any case, are *lagging* indicators? *Yikes!*

Now, a word about measurement, because I can hear you protesting that it's awfully hard to quantify Stakeholder Commitment. It is possible, and frequently beneficial, to measure without significant precision. We do it all the time.

If you are driving in winter and are coming to a curve, you "measure" the road conditions to determine if the surface is ice-covered or bare. You don't need to know the specific coefficient of friction between your tires and the road surface to decide whether you need to slow down. And yet, the road condition is your leading indicator for successful navigation of the curve.

So back to our matrix, and our big question. As a program

or project manager, where are you going to "up your game" in measuring, tracking, and managing a successful outcome? What does that look like? And whom do you look like, as a leader, not just a manager?

Great questions.

WHAT SEPARATES "EXPERT" PROJECT/PROGRAMME MANAGERS FROM THE REST?

The Dreyfus scale of expertise, from Level One to Level Five, is well established scientifically and is widely used. Lia DiBello, CEO of WTRI, and a published cognitive scientist, has studied the phenomenon of expertise as it manifests in project managers, through interviews and behavioral studies in a wide range of practitioners. She has clearly demonstrated that the key distinguishing behaviors with Level Five accomplished veterans is that they manage stakeholders well, and they know who the "real" stakeholder is. They manage projects in such a way as to provide the hoped for business benefits, even if the project plan, strictly executed, would not do that. They know when to make changes and have the ability to sell the changes to stakeholders. When difficulties arise – even major ones – they are able to look at these events as opportunities for greater results rather than as insurmountable problems or risks to be avoided.

Relationship management, leadership, and a laser focus on business benefits – these are the competencies that separate the best from the rest.

And this comes as no surprise, against the backdrop of the Seven Keys To Success. The most critical dimensions relate to Stakeholder Commitment, Business Benefit Realization, and creating a High Performing Team.

Here's the rub, though. Most PM training focuses on planning, tracking, and containing scope.

Appropriate behaviors for Level 3 PM expertise, for sure. Unfortunately, somewhere between irrelevant and counter-intuitive to Level 5 performance.

So the question is: what are companies doing to develop the most important competencies in those who lead their most important projects and programmes?

Perhaps the answer sheds a different light on why we still can't seem to get beyond a failure rate of 60-70% of projects.

HOW WILL DATA ANALYTICS, COGNITIVE COMPUTING, AND SOCIAL MEDIA CHANGE THE NATURE OF PROJECT MANAGEMENT?

It has been perversely comforting over the last 30 years to see that success or failure in managing projects is still determined by the same issues. Indeed, The Seven Keys To Success framework, when it was conceived 20 years ago, explained the fundamental basis for success or failure of every project in the previous 10 years of history of Coopers & Lybrand Consulting as well as Price Waterhouse Consulting. It has been in widespread use continuously since then in PwC Consulting and now in IBM, and has helped many Project Managers successfully navigate challenging engagements. And yet there also remain too many times that outcomes are not successful. Inevitably, the reasons – and the missed opportunities that would have altered the course of history - are always understandable against that framework.

As I say, perversely comforting.

And yet there are some seismic tremors being felt in the world of technology-driven projects that have even this old dog thinking he may need to learn some new tricks. I remain convinced that the Seven Keys will continue to be relevant. What I am curious about is how these phenomena – Data Analytics, Cognitive Computing, and Social Media for Business – might significantly change the landscape over which our projects are conceived and executed.

Let's start with Data Analytics and Cognitive Computing. These aren't just enabling technologies. This is an opportunity to profoundly change businesses – including the business of government – by <u>inventing</u> new benefits arising from merging and analyzing multiple sources of input, some of which are static, but many of which are processed in real time or near-real time, and applying cognitive computing to make the human element so much more powerful. Current examples include smarter cities such as Rio de Janeiro. Other examples can be found in smarter health care with personal monitors that send data in near-real time for pattern diagnostics and alerts to health care providers. What impact would those kinds of projects have on our notion of methods, of business benefit realization, of the breadth of stakeholder landscapes, and of mitigating technical risks?

Now consider social media. Beyond the Big Data aspects (e.g. mining Twitter and Google traffic for behavioral patterns), I am intrigued by the prospects that might arise from crowd sourcing. How might a project engage a much broader set of stakeholders to understand requirements or test user interfaces using social media? How might a project team find and test technical solutions using social media? Will this, in fact, become the next wave in the realm of knowledge management? Who needs to capture knowledge artifacts in searchable databases if you can connect in real time to the right mind?

Whatever the future of projects and project management bring, I am pretty confident that it will be quite different from the typical project of today.

I'm also pretty confident that five or ten years from now I will still find our collective track records of success perversely comforting.

WHAT CAN YOU LEARN FROM THE SCHOOL OF VIRTUAL KNOCKS?

All the really good (read "expert") project managers I know or have heard of have become so through years of experience, through which they have gained as much scar tissue as they have wisdom.

Must it always be so? Perhaps not.

Lia DiBello has published a post on the WTRI website titled "Project management expertise in weeks instead of years; the results are in." Admittedly, this article does not purport to create experts (Level 5 on the Dreyfus scale of expertise). But it does claim that it moved a number of participants from Novice or Advanced Beginner (Levels 1 and 2) to Intermediate or Competent (Levels 3 and 4). This acquisition of expertise in real life can typically require 10 years or more, not to mention at what cost of any failures or errors committed along the way.

Interestingly, when I mentioned this to a group of highly experienced consultants and project managers, most of whom were in their 40's and early 50's, my "news" was met with extreme skepticism. When I probed a bit deeper, the negative reaction stemmed from the perceived threat that their hard-won expertise might be discounted in the job market if younger people could come along so quickly and easily.

I imagine old-time airplane pilots scoffed at the first flight simulators too. Yet professional training at the highest levels now requires their use. Schools of Medicine and Nursing require training on simulated patients too, by the way.

I wonder when project management organizations are going to catch up? I wonder how many untimely "crashes" and "deaths" might be saved?

WHAT IF YOU COULD ACCELERATE "TIME TO WISDOM"?

What does it take to acquire deeper expertise in project management? To build wisdom beyond simply learning skills? Too often, this takes years of experience, often at significant cost to the enterprise when the wisdom gained by the individual comes at the expense of significant failure at the enterprise level.

One company – WTRI - has a proven approach to developing this expertise using virtual world technology, driven by an underlying engine that simulates complex business and real world events, and that is structured in accordance with principles from the field of cognitive science. The impact is to create a "safe-fail" environment wherein people can first un-learn the limitations of their current thinking and perspective and consequently try different approaches that measurably migrate them upward toward a level of "intuitive expert". And all within a couple of months, not years, and with no real cost of failing, which is so cognitively necessary to this kind of learning.

How does this actually work?

WTRI has built its own proprietary virtual world, coupled to its proprietary event generator. The result is a virtual world as big as the world itself and one that embodies the dynamic economic models of the world and of companies. It can be as complex as it needs to be, without the typical constraint to online learning of highly scripted and overly simplified scenarios.

The projects are located in companies that – while fictional – are fully fleshed out in terms of their finances, products, history and technologies. The companies are located in a world economy that – while fictional – is fully fleshed out with the issues facing global and multi-national companies today, such as integrating supply chains and managing regulatory constraints.

It is just this kind of complexity that separates "expert" project managers from the rest. The Dreyfus scale of expertise, from Level One to Level Five, is well established scientifically and is widely used. With respect to project managers, Level Five accomplished veterans manage stakeholders well, and they know who the "real" stakeholder is. They manage projects in such a way as to provide the hoped for business benefits, even if the project plan, strictly executed, would not do that. They know when to make changes and have the ability to sell the changes to stakeholders. When difficulties arise – even major ones – they are able to look at these events as opportunities for greater results rather than as insurmountable problems or risks to be avoided.

Each team of participant learners gets two attempts at the exercise, in accordance with the cognitive science precept that failure is very important to accelerating learning. Participants who are not operating at the expert level will miss the big picture on the first try and will not achieve successful results. After a debrief, they are given a second chance, with some programmed additional challenges to the events within and outside the project.

In this second pass, by focusing on key relationships and ultimate business outcomes, they inevitably perform at a Dreyfus level which is measurably higher than where they began before the first pass, as assessed in three ways:

- The financial success or the business benefits delivered by the project; there were the expected business benefits, which were not easy to actualize given the complexity of the project, but which could also be exceeded if the project managers identified hidden opportunities
- The Seven Keys, a "project health" metric developed by PWC and IBM Global Business Services; both the team and the stakeholders rate the project multiple times on seven critical dimensions and discuss any discrepancies in their perspectives
- A set of 30 challenges that elicit "judgments" that measure the team's Dreyfus level.

In documented outcomes, some participants who began at Level Two reached Level Four on the Dreyfus scale on many of the challenges. To put this in context, Human Resource data shows that moving from a Level Two to a Level Four in performance would normally take from 10-15 years, depending on opportunities, leadership and types of experiences.

There are many "distance learning" technologies and sponsoring companies, many of which are focused on project managers. None, however, have the measurable impact that WTRI achieves with its unique blend of virtual worlds, realistic and complex business simulation, and the application of the principles of cognitive science.

WTRI's solution creates a significant shift - in expertise not merely skills, in months not years, without the cost of failure.

What is that worth?

REFLECTIONS ON LEARNING

I will leave you with one final question to ponder. There are many ways in which to divide the world into two kinds of people. Some of those ways affect the lives of professionals, project managers, and organization leaders. These include those who are introverts and those who are extroverts, those who care about punctuality and those who don't, and those who focus on process (the analytics) and those who focus on outcomes (drivers).

There is one other important way in which you can think about two kinds of people. There are those who interact with others for the primary purpose of confirming their thinking. And there are those who interact with others in anticipation of changing their thinking.

In the world of professional development, there is a well-known model for learning:

- To change business performance, you must change behavior
- To change behavior, you must change thinking
- To change thinking, you must change beliefs and assumptions.

And so, we try to design belief-changing professional development events as a powerful way of creating deep learning and impacting business performance. If you truly want to learn and grow, it seems you may be required to let go of some of what you think and believe. Are you ready – and willing – to change your mind?

www.ingramcontent.com/pod-product-compliance
Lightning Source LLC
Chambersburg PA
CBHW021922170526
45157CB00005B/2145